DON'T PAN

(A Guide to Whelping, Rearing and Selling Puppies)

by

Wendy Lewis

Copyright 2003
WENDY LEWIS

The right of Wendy Lewis to be identified as author of this work has been asserted by her in accordance with Copyright, Designs and Patents Act 1988.

All rights reserved. No reproduction, copy or transmission of this publication may be made without written permission.

No paragraph of this publication may be reproduced, copied or transmitted save with the written permission or in accordance with the provisions of the Copyright Act 1956 (as amended).

Any person who does any unauthorised act in relation to this publication may be liable to criminal prosecution and civil claims for damage.

All characters in this publication are fictitious and any resemblance to real persons, living, or dead, is purely coincidental.

Foreword by
P.J. LARKIN.   DR. MED VET M.R.C.V.S.

No two breeders have precisely the same views on whelping and rearing puppies.

Wendy Lewis has her own ideas, and with ten years of experience to back them up, they are sound, practical and sensible. She manages very happily to steer her way through the maze of conflicting opinion to produce a little book that will be invaluable, not only to newcomers in her own breeds, but to many more experienced owners.

No-one knows everything about rearing puppies, and this, as a guide to read while you're waiting for that final push, may well have something for most owners.

I particularly welcome the important advice on selling your puppies.

Peter Larkin.

CONTENTS

INTRODUCTION
THE STUD DOG
THE MATING
CARE OF THE PREGNANT BITCH
WHELPING EQUIPMENT
THE WHELPING
PUPPY REARING
WEANING
WORMING
SELLING PUPPIES

DON'T PANIC

A Guide to Whelping, Rearing and Selling Puppies.

The following information is based on my personal experience of whelping around thirty litters of Dachshunds and Lancashire Heelers. All theories and opinions expressed in this book are my own and evolve from the above experience; others will have reared very successful litters using quite different methods.

Before embarking on breeding a litter of puppies it is as well to ask yourself one or two questions; bearing in mind the fact that most dog rescue homes are overflowing with unwanted dogs, many of whom have been cruelly treated.

Why do you want a litter? If the answer is ' because it would be good for the bitch,' then do not bother to mate her. She will be perfectly happy as long as you love and care for her, and she will never realise that she has missed anything.

Another frequently heard reason is that 'it will settle the bitch down.' It won't. I have never known having a litter to change a bitch's basic temperament. A jittery, sharp bitch will probably become fiercer when all her protective instincts are aroused.

Do NOT embark on a litter if you are not going to be at home all day to care for them. Many things could go disastrously wrong while you are away.

Rearing a litter is time consuming and expensive: don't expect to make money out of it. There are many hidden costs such as vets bills, electricity, soap powder etc.

DO make sure you have some homes lined up for your puppies... genuine ones. You will find that most of the friends and relatives, who would "love one of dear Flossy's puppies," suddenly find good reasons why they can't have one when your puppies are four to five weeks old. They tend to move house or leave the country, or find some member of the family who is allergic to dogs.

Having established that your reasons for breeding a litter are sound, and that you have the time to devote to the exercise, you will be looking for a Stud dog.

THE STUD DOG

A fair amount of consideration should be given to your choice of a Stud dog. It is not a good idea to rush to the top winning dog in your breed, unless he carries the characteristics which will compliment those of your bitch and, hopefully, produce puppies which are as good as, or better than, their parents.

It is of vital importance that the dog of your choice should be of sweet, amenable temperament. It is very unlikely that many of the resulting litter will enter the show ring, therefore most of them will become pets. The prime qualities for a pet should be a sound healthy animal of good temperament, with no inherited abnormalities.

The quick way to the top in the show ring, seems to be to mate close relatives to 'fix' type. This can work, but it will also accentuate any faults, seen or unseen, and does tend to reduce the size of the animal.

A mating of distant relatives is called Line-Breeding. A mating of close relatives such as Father/Daughter or Brother/Sister is called In-Breeding and should only be undertaken by very knowledgeable people, and even then is of very doubtful value.

I have mated a Father to a Daughter in a breed where everything in the pedigrees was a complete outcross. The result was two dogs and two bitches. One dog was very small and highly strung. The other, though very nice was a unilateral cryptorchid (only one testicle descended). One bitch which was humanely destroyed at two days old, and on post mortem was found to have a deformed intestine. The other bitch had the worst overshot mouth I have ever seen. This litter definitely put me off breeding with closely related dogs.

I started to breed dogs in an old established breed, and after five years had managed to acquire most of the inherited faults of that breed - after quite a good start.

Eventually, although I could produce dogs which would win in the show ring, I did not want to breed from them because I knew there were faults in other members of the same litter. Also, the Kennel Club Breed Standard for this breed (dachshunds) read 'long, low and level' which is nice alliteration but is a recipe for spinal problems, severe pain for the dogs, and much heartache for owners.

Over a period, loving pet homes were found for most of my small kennel of dachshunds (the oldies stayed with me), and I took up a newly recognised rare breed which had not been inbred and was still full of hybrid vigour.

At the first Breed show I attended, out of the thirty dogs entered, only two or three looked alike. In the fifteen years in which I have been watching this breed, the dogs are beginning to conform much more to a standard, but problems have now arisen because in the early days too many bitches were mated to one top winning dog.

Although this produced very nice-looking puppies, it has now reduced the gene pool significantly, which has resulted in a lack of good sires which could be used as an outcross.

Anyway, back to your Stud dog, chosen we hope for his good temperament as well as his beauty.

Contact the dog's owner BEFORE your bitch comes into season and make the arrangements for her to visit him. If you do not already know it, ask for a copy of the dog's pedigree which you can then compare with your bitch's.

When your bitch comes into season, worm her, but do not worm her again after she has been mated until about four weeks after the birth of her puppies.

If you keep several bitches, you may find that they will all come into season at around the same time. If this happens, keep a close eye on any unmated bitch whose season coincided with your pregnant bitch. The unmated one may probably show signs of having milk about eight weeks after her season, and should anything go wrong with your whelping it may be possible to stimulate her milk to foster the puppies.

A very maternal Miniature Dachshund of mine, who was busy guarding an imaginary litter in her bed, reared, very successfully, five Standard Dachshund puppies for a friend whose bitch had picked up rat poison and died the night she had the puppies.

In packs of wild dogs it is natural for unmated bitches to produce milk and feed the puppies while the dam is out hunting.

Inform the stud dog's owner when your bitch first comes in season and arrange the date for her visit: this will usually be eleven or twelve days after you have first noticed she is bleeding.

If you have to travel a long way to the dog of your choice, the twelfth day may be the best. If you can manage two matings, do them on the tenth and twelfth days. That way you should have viable sperm in the bitch for a period of four days.

If you keep other dogs, your bitch will show when she is ready to be mated, by flirting with them and standing with her tail curled over to one side, inviting them to mount her.

THE MATING

It is usual practice for the bitch to travel to the dog's home for the mating. On arrival, the first thing you should do is take her for a short walk in case she needs to empty herself.

Then, if she hasn't taken an instant dislike to the dog, allow them a short period of flirtation, off the lead if possible, to relax her. Not too long or the dog may 'run out of puff'.

If she does decide she hates him, one can achieve a mating with a keen dog by tying the bitch's mouth with a bandage, to stop her biting, and holding her firmly for the dog. Large breeds may present more of a problem. A diffident dog may be put off completely by a snapping and snarling bitch.

I am not really in favour of rape in these cases. I have done it, but things have tended to go wrong at the other end of the pregnancy.

One owner and I spent most of a day trying to mate her reluctant bitch to one of my stud dogs, and finally achieved it in the evening. She duly whelped two puppies, but the bitch died two days later.

Another bitch which I had mated against her will had a long, protracted whelping which was really a case of partial inertia. After these two experiences, if any bitch was adamant that she didn't want to be mated, I decided to trust to her instinct that she knew things that I didn't.

Sometimes a bitch will accept one dog quite happily but refuse another, again there is probably a very good reason why, so I don't force the issue.

Presuming all is going well, the dog will mount the bitch and they will tie. Once tied, the dog may turn so that they face away from each other. This is probably a defensive measure should they be attacked whilst relatively helpless. At least there are two sets of teeth facing outwards.

They will remain tied throughout the mating. Usually a tie last for about twenty minutes, it can be shorter. It can also be much longer: I had two dogs once which tied for two and a half hours during which time the dog went to sleep twice. I had to break it up eventually by putting towels under the dogs and pouring cold water on the relevant bits.

The first part of the dog's ejaculate carries the sperm, and the subsequent fluid washes it through. Consequently it is perfectly possible to get a pregnancy if the pair do not tie, provided the dog has entered the bitch for a minute or two.

It is best to gently hold both dogs steady whilst they are tied. A jittery bitch could possibly harm the dog and I know of one dog which died of a ruptured spleen after mating a difficult bitch.

After the mating, the stud dog's owner should give you a copy of the dog's pedigree which you will need in the future to write out the pedigrees for your puppies. You should also be given a Kennel Club Litter Registration form with the stud dog's section completed, giving his Kennel Club registration number.

The dog's owner should give you a receipt for the stud fee. Most owners will offer a free return to that dog if your bitch does not become pregnant, but this is not obligatory. What you are paying for is the actual mating on the day and the stud fee is not returnable if your bitch does not become pregnant.

Should this happen, it is most unlikely to be the stud dog's fault. Some bitches do not follow the usually accepted norm of being at maximum fertility on day eleven or twelve of their season. I have had one which became pregnant from an unplanned mating on day two, and another on day twenty two, when it should have been safe to let her back in with the pack; but this is unusual.

CARE OF THE PREGNANT BITCH

About three weeks after the mating, your bitch may seem to be a little 'off colour', which will be a promising sign that she is pregnant. You should be able to confirm this at about five weeks as, when viewed from above, she will be seen to be thickening at the waistline. At seven weeks you should be able to see and feel the pups move.

Birth normally takes place on or about the 63rd day of pregnancy. There is remarkably little variation in this gestation length, therefore if your bitch goes more than two days over this time, you should seek veterinary advice in case there is a problem.

During the pregnancy, follow exactly the same routine and feed the bitch as you did before. Don't start adding all sorts of exotic foods and vitamin pills to her diet; you are in danger of doing more harm than good. If she has always looked fit and well on her normal diet, then stick to it. Her body has enough to do with adjusting to the pregnancy, without having to cope with unfamiliar foods.

The most important thing with the breeding of any animals is to observe them carefully. If they look bright eyed, fit and well in their coats, they are getting all they need.

Keep up the exercise right until the day she whelps. She will naturally slow up a bit towards the end, but all my bitches have come on normal walks all the way through pregnancy.

This can also be quite a good guide to when she is about to whelp. You will find that she is not keen to go far from home the day before she goes into labour and will try to go back to where she has decided to produce her litter.

Try to fix in the bitch's mind, at least a week before the puppies are due, that the whelping box is the best place to have them. Under the garden shed can give you heart failure and if she gets it into her head that your bed is ideal, you may have a hectic whelping chasing her upstairs every time there is a puppy coming; even when they are all born and nicely settled in the whelping box, you will find she still keeps going back to the place where SHE had decided to have them.

Around the fifth to sixth week of pregnancy you can increase the bitch's daily food ration by about ten percent, unless she is too fat anyway, in which case it is best to use the pregnancy to slim her a bit. A lean fit bitch will have an easier, quicker, whelping than a fat lazy one. The fat one will have layers of fat internally as well as externally, and this will impede the passage of the pups and make the uterus sluggish.

The sixth to seventh week increase the ration again by ten percent, and so on each week until she whelps. Don't overdo the food in the last two weeks as this is when the pups really begin to grow, and enormous pups will give a difficult whelping.

Every day for the last week prior to whelping give the bitch calcium tablets, dosing according to size. This is to try to ensure that there will be enough calcium in the system for the actual birth. Remember she has had to use calcium to build the puppies' skeletons. After she has whelped, increase the dose, spreading it over the day, all the time that she is producing milk for the puppies. This is to try to prevent Eclampsia, which can be a killer.

ECLAMPSIA is caused by a sudden demand on the bitch's calcium supply resulting in her depriving herself of her own blood calcium to put into the milk. This usually happens after the puppies are born, but I do know of someone who lost a bitch with it the day before she should have whelped seven puppies. The owner didn't realise what was wrong.

SYMPTOMS OF ECLAMPSIA are as follows:-
The bitch will seem unhappy and uncomfortable and may start to pant. Her head may begin to shake like someone

with Parkinsons disease. She may go lame or off her legs altogether. If you put a hand on her you will be able to feel her muscles jumping and twitching.

IT IS VITAL THAT YOU TAKE HER STRAIGHT TO THE VET no matter the time of day or night, or she will die.

Depending on how far the Eclampsia has progressed the vet will either give her two calcium injections; one intramuscular for a more rapid effect, and another subcutaneous one for long acting effect. If the bitch is in danger of going into convulsions, which is the next stage, the vet will administer an intravenous injection of calcium which can have an almost magically instantaneous effect, though don't worry if it doesn't.

If you have gone straight to your vet at the first signs of eclampsia, your bitch has every chance of surviving, but do not waste any time in doing so.

Your vet may then suggest that you take the bitch away from the puppies and hand rear them. This is fine in theory but virtually impossible in practice as your bitch will be utterly miserable and make sure that you are too.

I compromise, until the pups are eating and drinking by themselves at around four weeks, by leaving the bitch with them but watching her like a hawk all day, and either having her in my bed at night, with two trips out to feed the puppies; or sleeping fitfully on a mattress on the floor beside the whelping box. It's exhausting, but doesn't go on for long.

A clear whitish discharge from the vulva may be seen during the last few weeks of pregnancy, this is normal and nothing to worry about. Should you at any stage of the pregnancy see a black or greenish discharge you will need veterinary assistance as, probably,
one of the puppies has died in the uterus.

WHELPING EQUIPMENT

1) Whelping Box (well disinfected)
2) Newspapers.
3) Two Vet Beds. (Special synthetic furry washable pads)
4) Dull Emitter Heat Lamp.
5) Heated Pad.
6) Pair of Blunt Scissors.
7) Artery Clamp.
8) Sewing cotton & Iodine.
9) Several Towels and a flannel.
10) Cardboard Box.
11) Hot Water Bottle.

FINALLY, and probably most important, a large flask of hot coffee. Veterinary advice on this is that the flask should also contain brandy.

The Whelping Box should be large enough to give the bitch and pups room to move about. Ideally it should be possible to have the sides low for the actual delivery so that one can reach the bitch comfortably should assistance be needed. Then the sides will need to be heightened (or perhaps another box) so that it can be covered and darkened for two or three weeks after the pups are born.

This makes the box warmer, draught free and nearer to the natural conditions of earth or cave which the bitch would have chosen for herself. When whelping is imminent take care that she doesn't disappear under the garden shed which may have to be dismantled to retrieve her.

The Whelping Box should have a wooden rail round the inside measuring 2.5cm x 2.5cm (1in x 1in.) This is fixed to the side of the box on blocks so that it projects into the box by about 5 cm.(2 in) at a height of about 7.5 cm (3 in) from the floor of the box. This will ensure that when the pups creep round behind their mum, as they invariably do during the first week of life, they will not be suffocated by her lying on them.

Place a pad of newspaper on the floor of the box and cover this with a piece of Vet Bed cut to fit the box. During the whelping I use a Dull Emitter Heat lamp over the box because it is useful for warming slow puppies as you are massaging life into them. The newspaper will soak up any fluid which will pass straight through the Vet Bed.

When whelping is completed, remove the newspaper, change to a heated pad under a clean Vet Bed and remove, or switch off the overhead Dull Emitter Lamp unless it is particularly cold. If leaving it on do make sure that there is a cool part of the box which the bitch and whelps can escape to if they get too hot.

The Blunt Scissors are for severing tough umbilical cords. Sharp scissors give too clean a cut which tends to bleed more. Remember this job is usually done by the bitch's teeth.

The Artery Clamp is to clamp to the afterbirth end of the cord if the afterbirth is still retained by the bitch after you have detached the puppy. This will hold the afterbirth and stop it slipping back into the uterus until the bitch is ready to deliver it easily.

The Towels are for drying puppies, and the Flannel for holding slippery puppies for an assisted delivery.

The Cardboard Box containing the Hot Water Bottle with a folded Vet Bed on top is for the first born pups to keep them warm and safe while the next one arrives...as long as the bitch does not mind you removing them. Don't have a battle with her over this; if she gets very distressed when you move them, it is safer to leave them with her and take the small risk of them getting stepped on. You can usually sneak them away just as the next one is appearing and taking all her attention.

THE WHELPING

I am not going to go into all the possible problems which can arise during a whelping as there are plenty of books which describe these. Most of them require veterinary assistance which you will have summoned when you felt that things were not proceeding normally; but I would just mention INERTIA.

If your bitch has reached her due date but nothing seems to be happening do not let her go more than two days past that date without having her checked by the vet. Sometimes, if there are only one or two puppies, they may not produce enough of the hormone needed to trigger the fall in progesterone levels to precipitate the whelping.

In cases of inertia you can usually detect subtle changes in your bitch if you know her well. I have known one who just sat around looking worried.

There can also be partial inertia where the bitch's body is not really working hard enough to expel the puppies. Although she may be having visible muscular contractions, the uterus may not be contracting. This could be caused by the bitch being overweight and under-exercised. There is also a school of thought that believes it could be an hereditary problem. It is as well before breeding from your bitch to ask for a history of her dam's whelping.

I cannot stress too much, how important it is to have your bitch lean and fit before the mating. It can save a lot of later problems. If your bitch is too fat it is better to put off having a litter for six months and work on her fitness during that time.

If you think that whelping is imminent, but are not sure, your best course is to take the bitch's temperature. The foetuses determine the time of whelping by triggering a fall in the level of the hormone progesterone in the bitch. This in turn causes a drop in the body temperature. This lowering of temperature normally occurs 24 to 48 hours before the bitch goes into labour. The normal temperature of 101.5 will drop to around 98 degrees.

The bitch will most probably go off her food and begin to scratch up her bedding to make a nest. If you sit and watch her flanks at this stage you may be able to see the horns of the uterus contracting into a hard ridge, while she bed-makes to take her mind off the pain. The pups lie in the horns of the uterus which run up each side of the bitch's flanks.

She will not have begun to push yet as the cervix will not be dilated enough to deliver the puppies. She may also be sick at this stage of the proceedings.

There will be a discharge of mucus: this is the plug which sealed the neck of the womb, coming away.

As soon as the cervix is fully opened, the bitch will go into the second stage of labour and will begin to push with each contraction. This stage seems to bother them less than the first and once they settle down to work, they seem to know what to expect at the end of it.

Look at your watch when you see the first actual push by the bitch. Most books on the subject will say that if you have not got a puppy in two hours from that time you may need assistance. If you bitch is a maiden and the straining seems normal with rests in between, and she is not too distressed I generally wait a little longer... it rather depends how far from your vet you live.

It is a good idea to let your vet know anyway when your bitch goes into labour so that he is primed should you need him later. As a matter of courtesy, don't forget to let him know afterwards that all has gone well.

If the bitch is straining continuously and seems in a lot of pain, after two hours without producing anything, something may be wrong.

At some stage the first water bag will appear and after a push or so will burst. Do not touch or burst this yourself as it is designed to gently dilate the passage for the puppies. You may not see this but will find the bitch is very interested in a wet patch in the bed.

The next water bag to appear should contain a puppy, there is a water bag with each puppy. You will see the end of the bag appear. Do not touch it or interfere at all. Quite often if the pup is half out, the urge to help may be overwhelming. But control this urge. A few more pushes will deliver the pup naturally, whereas if you pull it you may hurt the bitch and she will probably stop pushing and may even try to get out of the whelping box to get away from the pain.

The time to assist the birth is usually if you can see that the pup is coming backwards; that is with the tail and hind feet showing. This presentation is not unusual but may take the bitch longer to push out. Don't interfere unless you think she is really struggling to get it out.

In all the litters I have delivered, just under half the pups were posterior presentation. This is not a breech birth.

A breech birth is when you are presented with the pup's bottom only with the hind legs still forward. I have never had this situation, but would suggest that you wait until the bitch stops pushing, then between pushes, try to ease the pup back inside her, find the back legs, and bring them back into the correct position.

When assisting a posterior presentation, take hold of what you can of the pup with a clean flannel, (they are very slippery) and as the bitch pushes, ease the pup, very gently, in a curve, down, round and underneath the bitch between her hind legs. This is the natural direction for the birth.

Never pull straight out; and don't pull when the bitch is not straining.

Most of all DON'T PANIC: it won't help; the bitch will sense it and it will take her mind off the job.

When the pup is delivered, you can leave the bitch to free it from the membrane if she seems to know what to do. I must admit here that I don't...all that chewing and pulling on the umbilical cord worries me, and can leave your pups with umbilical hernias. I lost a pup once with peritonitis because the bitch had chewed the cord off right against the pup and infection had set in.

Some bitches seem to start chewing through the cord before freeing the pup from the membrane and become more interested in the afterbirth, leaving the pup struggling to breathe with its head still enclosed in the membrane.

If this happens, tear the membrane away from the head with your fingers and wipe the nose and mouth then, if the pup is still attached to the bitch by the cord, (the afterbirth still not having come away from the bitch) use the Artery Clamp, clamping it onto the cord about 2.5 cm (2 ins) away from the pup, being careful not to pull the cord where it is attached to the navel.

Also be very careful not to pinch the skin of the bitch's vulva with the clamp.

The reason for using the clamp is to stop the afterbirth slipping back into the bitch when you free the puppy.

Next break the cord using either, finger nails (clean), or a blunt pair of scissors. A ragged tear is more natural and bleeds less, if at all. If the bleeding does not stop almost immediately, tie the end of the cord with a piece of cotton soaked in iodine, but do not do this if it is not really necessary.

If the pup and the afterbirth both come away together, leave breaking the cord for a minute or two to allow the blood in the placenta to drain into the pup. Making sure the pup is breathing properly is more important than detaching it in this case.

If the pup is being a bit slow to get going and the bitch is being very possessive about it you can distract her by cutting the cord and giving her the afterbirth to eat. This is natural for her and is a valuable food source.

Let her have the pup back as soon as you are sure it is all right. If its breathing seems a bit 'snuffly', as may well be the case if it has been born hind feet first and inhaled some fluid, hold it head down, but well supported and swing it gently from side to side to drain it.

Then let the bitch finish stimulating it, which she will do by licking it and pushing it about. It looks rough but doesn't seem to do them any harm.

The second pup may arrive fairly soon after the first, then there may be a longer wait between the second and third, or third and fourth. This is presuming a litter of three, four or five pups. This pause is usually due to the fact that during a normal whelping, one horn of the uterus empties first and the pause seems to cover the change over to the other horn starting to contract.

This pause can be used to make sure that the pups have had their first feed. Their suckling will stimulate the next lot of contractions.

This feed is most important as the first milk contains Colostrum which carries the antibodies which will give the pups protection against disease for the first few weeks of their lives. They are much less likely to get sick at the early stage than when they reach seven or eight weeks old when this immunity from the dam begins to wear off. The puppy's gut is only permeable by the Colostrum for a few hours so it is very important to make sure that each one of them has had a good feed as soon as possible.

They may be lying close up against the bitch and look as if they are feeding, but do check that they are latched on and sucking.

If the bitch seems to be having a bit of a rest after producing a couple of pups, offer her a drink of warm milk with a teaspoon of glucose and a crushed calcium tablet in it.

Don't forget that she may well want to relieve herself after the whelping, especially if she has had a couple of drinks during this time. If she doesn't settle after the last pup has been born, this may well be all that is wrong with her.

You will have to take her outside as she will be very reluctant to leave the pups. TAKE A TORCH with you if it is dark, there may be another pup yet to come and it won't be the first to be born on the lawn.

Never see the first couple of pups into the world and then go to bed leaving the bitch to 'get on with it'. You may come down in the morning to 'stillborn' pups which need not have been with a little timely assistance from you...or even a dead bitch. There are many things which can go wrong even after two normal deliveries.

You have planned the mating, paid the stud fee and waited for nine weeks for this event: one night's lost sleep is not a lot to sacrifice and you owe it to your bitch to care for her properly.

After the last pup has been born, presuming all has gone normally, the bitch should settle down to washing and feeding her litter. If she still seems restless there may be one more pup to come, probably from higher up in the horn. I have had a puppy born eight hours after the other four. Unfortunately it was dead. This pup could probably have been saved by a caesarean section, but I was whelping the bitch for someone else and they would rather have lost the pup than subject their adored bitch to an operation.

In this case it was probably wise because it was very difficult to get this bitch to settle to her maternal duties anyway; if she had been confused by coming round from the anaesthetic, she may not have recognised them as her children.

If your bitch does have to have a caesarean, especially if she is a maiden, do make sure she has accepted the pups before you consider leaving her alone with them. A friend of mine came down in the morning to a whelping box covered with blood and mangled bodies, where the bitch in her confused state had killed all four pups after a caesarean delivery.

Getting back to your whelping. If you have seen the afterbirth from each pup as it was born, all well and good, but sometimes they do not come away with the pup and slip back inside the uterus.

If this does happen, bear it in mind whilst watching your bitch carefully for the next few days. Usually they break down and come away over the next few days as a brownish discharge, but they can cause infection with a consequent rise in temperature.

It is very important to take your bitch's temperature every day after the whelping until it returns to normal. It is usual for it to rise to around 102 degrees for a day or so. If it goes above this then some infection has set in and you will need to get a course of penicillin from your vet.

There are various types of penicillin, make sure that you get the one that it is safe to give to a nursing bitch. Any other kind may cause you to have 'fading puppies'.

Be very careful about giving any medicine to a pregnant or nursing bitch and always check with your vet first. If she should have to visit the vet with any illness during her pregnancy, remember to tell him that she is pregnant when he is prescribing medicine. Cortisone can cause abortions.

There is an increased risk of infection for a bitch and puppies in a kennel where a lot of litters are born. If you do get 'fading puppies' this could be due to a virus harboured by unhygienic conditions.

'Fading puppies' are those which just seem to give up. They stop feeding and resist all efforts to keep them alive. It is impossible to be germ free, but one can ensure minimum risk by disinfecting whelping boxes and boiling scissors etc. before use.

After all the pups are born, check them for any deformities such as hind dew claws or cleft palates, the last could be the cause if the pup seems unable to suckle. If you have a breed where it is accepted practice to remove all dew claws this should be done by the vet when the pups are two to three days old. If hind dew claws are missed until after this stage it will mean an operation under anesthetic later in life to take them off.

Do put Vet-Bed in the whelping box. The pups can move well on it, reaching their dam easily. There is nothing worse than watching the poor little things struggling and sliding about on slippery newspaper. 'Vet-Bed' will keep them warm and dry as the moisture goes straight through it.

PUPPY REARING

For three weeks you should need to do very little for the pups beyond ensuring that they are kept warm, draught free and quiet. Use a heated pad underneath part of the Vet-Bed, and keep the box covered to darken it. I am not much in favour of heat lamps, they tend to draw the cold air up so that the pups are in a permanent draught; consequently it is difficult to get the temperature correct.

If you do have to use a heat lamp, make sure that there is room in the whelping box for the pups and bitch to escape from the heat if necessary.

If the puppies are lying spaced out all round the box, they are too hot. If piled on top of one another they are too cold. A greenhouse thermometer placed on the Vet-Bed under the lamp will tell you if you are cooking them or not.

Correct temperature for them at the beginning of their lives should be around 87F. The following table is a guide to whelping box temperatures when rearing orphan pups, or when the bitch is not present:-

1st week...................91 - 86F
2nd week.................86 - 82F
3rd week..................82 - 79F
4th week..................79 - 75F

The bitch's mammary glands give off a lot of heat at this time and, unless it is freezing mid-winter, as long as she is with them, gentle heat from underneath is all the puppies need.

Their eyes will open naturally around twelve to fourteen days, do not try to assist this procedure. The retina is not developed at birth, but at four weeks their vision is as good as an adult's. They are also deaf at first, but are hearing at about two weeks and hearing as well as an adult at about four weeks.

Under normal circumstances the puppies should double their birth weight by about 10 days old.

If a puppy cries a lot during the first few days of life, especially if the bitch rejects it and pushes it away to a corner of the box, you are probably going to lose it. At this age there is very little the Vet can do. The bitch's instinct is nearly always right and I have learned to trust it.

I have lost four pups like this. One took too long before the vet and I managed to get it to breathe at birth, and suffered brain damage. This one was destroyed at two days old as it was crying miserably and seemed unable to suckle.

The second one, as I previously mentioned had peritonitis.

The third, which was crying and not feeding, I had put down, and on post mortem it was found to have a completely solid section of intestine, the rest of the intestine was deformed as well.

The fourth, which died at four days was found to have improperly inflated lungs.

Until a pup is born, the blood-supply from the dam by-passes the lungs, which are deflated. At the moment of birth, nature miraculously re-routes the blood supply through the lungs to allow them to inflate, and breathing to start. During whelping it is vitally important to make sure the pup is breathing properly before handing it back to the bitch.

All these puppies which had to be put down were despatched by my vet with an injection. I have heard some fairly horrific stories from other breeders who talk of drowning pups, or 'knocking them on the head'. This sickens me. Please have the job done painlessly by your vet.

About two weeks after the pups are born you may find that your bitch would like to be away from them at times. Please ensure that she can escape when she wishes.

At about three weeks, carefully cut the sharp tips off the pups claws or they will scratch the bitch while they are feeding. A pair or ordinary nail clippers are best for this job. Take great care not to cut too much off because you will cut through the vein which runs down the nail, causing it to bleed. This also hurts the puppies.

WEANING

When your puppies are four weeks old you can start offering them solid food in the shape of some minced beef once a day, about a teaspoonful for a small breed.

At the same time always keep a small dish of fresh water in the whelping box, you will find that they will drink from it. The dish needs to be heavy glass or earthenware to avoid being tipped up.

By the beginning of the fifth week they should be eating the meat well and you will have to increase the amount...I always feed to appetite.

This is the time when the bitch would naturally begin to wean them by regurgitating her food for them. I have had one who carried lumps of her own dinner into the box to offer them.

Having eaten her food, the bitch will probably go into the whelping box and stand while the pups suckle...after about a minute this will stimulate her to regurgitate her dinner into a corner of the box for them to eat; this is perfectly natural, your bitch is not ill or being sick.

At the age of five weeks, ease the puppies onto the same food that their dam eats. I do not agree with those who advise feeding dogs on Farex and other baby foods. These are designed for humans and are unsuitable for dogs.

Puppies never seem to have upset tummies at weaning when fed on the same food as their dams regular diet; after all this was what they were getting through the blood supply when they were in the womb, and subsequently through the milk supply, so their bodies are already adjusted to processing it.

Do not try to forcibly wean your puppies; as long as their dam will feed them, let her. They are still receiving antibodies through her milk supply.

Let her stay with them until they leave for their new homes and they will end up better behaved, having received a few sharp corrections from her for excessive biting or just generally being a nuisance.

A lot of temperament problems can be cured between five and eight weeks old when the puppies are very receptive to gentle but firm correction for excessive noise or bullying their brothers and sisters.

Weather-permitting, the puppies should now be spending some time outside in the fresh air.

Always make sure they have water and shade in their runs and don't forget that the sun moves round very quickly, and that a puppy up to the age of seven or eight weeks is not yet able to control its body temperature very efficiently.

Their bed should be in the shade as they will only play for about twenty minutes before needing some sleep.

WORMING

Worm the puppies when they are four weeks old, unless any of them have upset stomachs and loose motions. If this is the case, leave the worming until they are all better.

Consult your vet about suitable worming tablets for your breed. On some occasions I have found that the stated dose of a whole tablet can be rather a lot for a small breed; sometimes some of my puppies felt a bit poorly and brought up the tablet before it had had time to take effect, in which case I would give them half a tablet.

When you have dosed the puppies, keep the bitch away from them for four hours or so, or she may clear up after them and ingest a hefty dose of worms, and the worming medicine, herself. Leave worming the bitch until a week after you have done the puppies.

Dose the pups again at around seven weeks, using the same dose. You may not see any worms after this dose, probably the four week old worms were too immature to have laid eggs.

Bitches naturally clear up after their very young puppies and I have had several bitches feel unwell at around the four week period of rearing puppies, culminating in two or three days of sickness and diarrhoea. This is best treated by not allowing her to clear up, and by starving her for a day - just allowing her boiled water with natural organic honey in it.

When she feels well enough to eat again, offer her lightly scrambled egg, and if that stays down and she seems hungry, follow it up with boiled white fish and boiled white rice. Never try to force her to eat, starving is positively beneficial in these cases and she knows best what her body needs. Do NOT give her milk, it is not a natural food for an adult dog and it curdles in the stomach. She should, if possible, have access to some couch grass to help with internal cleansing.

SELLING PUPPIES

At eight weeks old your puppies should be ready to go to their new homes. As a responsible breeder you should have a few questions to ask of your prospective purchasers to ensure that your pups will have a long and happy life.

Genuine dog lovers don't mind being given the 'third degree' as they know it is for the dog's benefit.

Questions should be something on the following lines:-
1) Is there someone at home all day?
2) Do they have a safely fenced garden?
3   Do ALL members of the family want a dog?
4)   Are there any children under ten years old in the family?

If the puppy is to be a present for the child, I like to meet that child and see it with the puppy. Puppies are not toys, and unless the situation is handled very carefully, the puppy will probably attach itself to the lady of the house, which could upset the child and cause problems.

5) Are there any other dogs in the household, and if there are, what sex and breed. If the resident dog is very protective of its owners it may well resent a newcomer, even going to the lengths of killing it.

Never forget that the dog retains all its wild instincts underneath a thin veneer of our imposed civilization.

FINALLY...Please do not sell puppies just before Christmas. If people want them for Christmas presents; having ensured that it is a good home, keep the puppy until after the festivities have died down. It is hard enough on a puppy having to adjust to a new home without being pitched into a madhouse of people having parties and making a lot of noise, and with no-one having the time to settle the pup in gently.

People usually don't mind if you explain this to them, and if they do, they are probably not the right kind of prospective owner anyway.

Give your puppies a thorough examination when they are seven weeks old. Check them for dandruff, which can be removed by shampooing with the baby preparation Crado-Cap, obtainable from the chemist. Look into the ears and if they are dirty, treat them with drops which you can get from your vet. Do not put powder in their ears, it can set like concrete.

Look for signs of fleas, there are powders and shampoos which can be used on small puppies, but do check the labels on the bottles to confirm that they are suitable.

NEVER spray your dogs with an anti-flea preparation in an enclosed area, or confine them in a kennel after spraying. These sprays contain a nerve gas. Three retrievers, which were sprayed and then shut away together in their kennel, died from this gas.

Get all the paperwork done in advance...it is impossible to talk to the new owners when they come for the puppy, whilst writing out pedigrees and diet sheets.

The diet sheet should state exactly what you have fed the puppy and the times that it was fed. You can also help the puppy to settle into its new home by giving its normal rest times, and roughly when it has been used to going out to relieve itself.

Suggest to the new owners that they clean the pup's teeth fairly regularly...it has obviously never occurred to most of them that one can. There are special doggy toothpastes on the market. An ordinary toothbrush with the bristles cut down is quite suitable.

They should also not let the toenails grow too long if the dog is not getting enough roadwork to keep them short.

Remind them that their puppy is still a baby and will need a lot of sleep; in a quiet warm place that it knows as its own. Preferably not a basket, they are draughty and are liable to be chewed producing splinters, or one of those pretty foam creations; I have known them to disintegrate all over the kitchen overnight. A cardboard box is best, with an old blanket or some vet bed until the puppy has finished teething.

If the puppy has started its course of injections, the Vets Certificate should be given to the new owner.

Give a receipt for the purchase price and write any special arrangements on it. If the puppy is Kennel Club Registered, give the registration certificate.

Send the puppy off with enough of its regular food to cover the first few days, and a piece of blanket which it has been sleeping on with its brothers and sisters to see it through the first few lonely nights. Suggest to the new owners that they give it a warm hot-water bottle to cuddle up to.

Finally, all responsible breeders should offer to take back, or help to re-home a puppy if the purchaser can no longer keep it for any reason.

If your buyer is no longer in the first flush of youth try, tactfully, to get them to put in writing somewhere that, should anything happen to them, the dog will come back to you for re-homing. This will probably ensure that you are doubly careful where you place your pups so that they have good loving homes, and don't come bouncing back to you.

I have only had four returned to me in ten years, and all for perfectly acceptable reasons. It is a good idea to refund the purchase price, you may lose a little on the resale, but you will build up a lot of goodwill and hopefully know where the pups you have bred are at all times.

End

Printed in Great Britain
by Amazon